ACKNOWDLEGEMENTS

I would like to take the time out, to give praise to god.
I wouldn't have been able to do with out him, giving me the strength.
I also would like to thank all my day one supporters, you all pushed me for part two.
I have say to my children, I love you three boys with everything in me. Isayha my oldest son, your circumstances could be so much worse. You still have a life ahead of you. My middle child, you are such a smart boy. Follow your dreams, bring them to reality. Keep pushing and never give up. To my last son ramel junior, you are growing up way to fast, it seems like yesterday you were in my belly. Now you're in daycare, calling me mommy and calling daddy. I love you guys so much. I just want all three of you to know sky's the limit.

I want to say to my husband, you have giving me so much belief. You allowed me to explore my dreams. You pushed me two keep going, I am so thankful for you. You make me feel like nothing can stop me. Thank you, I love you so much. To my sister tracey, and Ericka, no matter what life have instore for our future with each other I am here always and forever. I love yall. To all my friends. I will come back with my hand, just except it. I also would like to give acknowledgement to my father-law thank you for always being there for me. Never give up! I did it so can you

DO EM DIRTY

PART 2   BY

IESHA HUGGINS

CHAPTER 1

Zamir said to Chica, "So you thought you would get away with that stunt you pulled huh?", then proceeded to pistol whip her. Chica was blind folded and her hands were tied. She remained calm trying to catch the voice talking, but she didn't know the voice. She was bleeding heavily, and was in a ton of pain. She was still hanging on though, with all the pain and blood pouring into eyes she still barked.

Take these blind folds off me bitch" Chica said with a wicked laugh. Zamir laughed at her response, even though she was beaten half to death she still had the heart of a lion. Wow "you still pretending to be a gangster even after this ass beating, I see" Zamir said chuckling. Well whoever you are I see you're a pussy ass bitch" hiding behind these blind folds you have on me, why don't you reveal your identity. Chica said spitting blood out her mouth. Don't worry little mama, my face will be revealed shortly just bear with me ok. I've waited a very long time for

8

this, you will finally realize I was the wrong bitch to play with. Zamir pistol whipped her, she was just tired of hearing her voice. Reyna didn't know what was going on. She didn't have on any blindfolds, she could see Zamir clear as day. She thought to herself, life for me is about to end. Why? What did I do she questioned herself? Zamir thought about what Candy told her to do. She looked at Reyna dead in her eyes, today life has just gotten better for you. Now you have only one option you little bitch, follow these simple instructions. However, if you

9

don't and you try saving this trifling bitch, you will

die in an instant. Now do I make myself clear Zamir

questioned? Reyna shook her head yes, and excepted

the envelope she was handed. Zamir slowly released

Reyna, she stood up and looked at her friend, her

sister she was thinking I have to help her. Lord I

cannot leave her. Zamir pointed the gun at her, you

can die right her and I mean it. Don't make me kill

you, clean your ass up and get the fuck out my face.

Zamir turned around and walked out the hotel room.

Stood in front and smoked a loose one, she didn't

10

believe Reyna was stupid enough to try her luck.

Reyna jotted out the bathroom to see if the mystery

girl left the room, she turned her head the mystery

woman was gone. She ran back in the bathroom,

omg Chica wake up she shook her repeatedly. Chica

looked up, noticing it was Reyna and spit blood on

the floor. Look Chica we are in some serious danger,

whoever this bitch is she has a real hard on for you. I

don't know why, but she letting me go. Chica finally

spoke, go don't try anything. I do have one question?

Where is she? She left the room Reyna cried. Listen

11

to me and really well. Find me something sharp, give

it to me and get the hell out of here. Do not worry

about me, I am a survivor, I will never be a victim

and die like this. looking at her Reyna hugged her

wiped her tears, I love you. Hey Chica called out,

Reyna turned around. Do em dirty. They both said.

Now go. Reyna slowly opened the door to the hotel

but there was no one insight. She looked around it

was clear. She thought about what the chick said and

she realized it was a set-up, she quickly thought

against it. turned back closed the door and left. She

12

slowly walked towards the elevator, Nah fuck that, I will not leave her to die. She stopped, then opened the envelope the chick gave her. Don't and I repeat turn back around. I know you, I also know you won't leave. Trust if I didn't care for you, you would already be dead. Please ray trust me, follow these instructions and no detours. Ray she thought, the only person who called her that was Candy. What the fuck she said to herself. She continued to stir at the letter, no she is dead. Nobody else called her ray beside peaches, and she was also dead. Something

13

was really wrong. Someone was playing dirty, real dirty. Why she screamed, she kneeled down. God, where are you? Where. I thought you kept your children safe she cried. Someone is about to kill my sister. You expect me to leave she yelled at the letter. You don't love me. Because you would know I love my sister. Who was calling her ray she tried hard to think. Fuck" this shit I refuse to leave my fucking sister. She took off running back to save her sister. She could care less about the consequences', sisters for life. She reached the hotel door and "boom" she

14

sent the door flying opened. What the fuck, the room was bloody. Chica, she ran towards the bathroom screaming. Blood was everywhere, yet the room was empty as ghost town. No, no, no. why did I leave her, why she yelled asking herself. She fucking dead cause of me. Yet she had to use her fucking brain, I know this bitch face she thought. "get the fuck out "bitch I know that face, I will find you. she looked both ways then took off in the opposite direction. As she made her exit, she realized she needed to get in touch with low. He would be able to tell her what to

15

do. Fuck" she didn't have a car, No money. How did life just turn around for the worse, without warning. She realized she could go back to the hotel, the clerk could help her. Heading back towards the hotel a car came at her full speed. She jumped and took a hard fall into the grass, are you shitting me" she looked up and three mask men proceeded jumping out the car and heading her direction. Oh shit" she tried to get up. Ugh, she was badly hurt. She tried again but it was too late. They swooped her up with force, and threw her into the car. She was quietly put to sleep.

16

By the time she would wake up, she would be at her destination.

CHAPTER TWO

18

Low was pasting back in forth, he was really about to lose his noodle. He hasn't buried his wife, peaches were murdered. Now the bitch who saved his life was in a coma. Are you shitting me, he said over and over in his head. He began to chuckle. He pulled out his phone and tried reaching the girls. Nah" what the hell is going on. Neither Reyna nor Chica was answering their phones. Ok, maybe they went out for food or drinks. He tried to reason with his self. He didn't have anyone to call for Latrice, there was no way he could call king. I'm going to kill this mother

19

fucker" he thought to his self. um yes excuse me he said stopping a nurse. Hello, how can I help you sir the lady nurse asked him. I would like to know if the young lady in room 232 has any other numbers to reach a loved one. I am just a friend. However, I have to go. but I need to make sure someone else can be reached before I leave. Well sir I am not really sure, however you can go give the front desk her information and have them take a look. Ok, thanks I appreciate it, low headed towards the nurse's station and he heard yelling coming from that direction. As he got closer his eyes grew wide, it was king demanding to see his sister. He wanted to kill "he knew he would never get away with killing king there. He thought quick, shit" king was heading in his direction. He sprinted in the opposite direction running into a doctor. What the hell" the doctor said as the items he had in his hand went flying. My fault doc, low said as he bent down helping pick the stuff up. King flew past low never noticing him, "woo" that was close low said out loud. Sir, this isn't a playground the doc said. Low look at the doc and

21

took off, he had to get the fuck out the hospital. He didn't know what the fuck was happening, what he did know was he would sit outside the hospital. and wait for king. He pulled out his phone and tried reaching the girls again. "fuck" he banged his hands against the stirring wheel, what is going on. He wondered, should he go back to the hotel. Nah he quickly shook that thought from his mind. His phone rung, not realizing the number he almost didn't answer. Yea he spoke into the receiver, help me. What? he said aloud the voice was low. Help me, help me. Chica he screamed, where are you he asked. I don't know, low scratched his head. Baby girl I'm going to need you to look around, tell me what you see. She wasn't responding. Chica stay with me, where is Reyna? She tried to speak but nothing would come out. She passed out from all the blood lost. What the fuck" he was losing it. This was a dream he couldn't wake up from. He started the engine and was about to go until he saw king and his crew coming out. Nah this mother fucker wasn't about to get away, he slid down and his seat and

23

waited. He was going to follow this bastard, he would see where he had his baby boy and get him back. King and his crew got into their cars and pulled out, low stayed back enough so he wouldn't get noticed. Thirty minutes later they pulled up to a house on Bleecker street just right outside of the city. Low noticed it was a nice house with picket fences. He wondered was his little man inside, he had to be cool even though he wanted to go in guns blazing. He knew that wouldn't be smart, he could fuck around and get his boy killed. It seemed like forever

24

just sitting there waiting, so he proceeded getting out

the car. He slowly looked around making sure there

were no hidden traps, he jumped the fence and

started towards the back of the house. He slowly

began looking into a window, he didn't see much.

He quickly went to the side window, and that is

when he saw king and his crew sitting and smoking.

He was in an outrage, he wanted blood. This

"bastard" he couldn't believe this "mother fucker" he

thought. nigga relaxing with his feet up he was going

to "kill this bitch ass" with his bare hands. King got

25

a phone call and walked out. Low watched the other guys laughing and joking, he now realized he needed help. He walked around the other side of house trying not to make a sound, dogs started barking. Shit, shit he said aloud. He took off as fast as he could, the dogs continued barking roof, roof. All the neighborhood lights came on. Surprisingly he made it to his car in flash, his heart was pumping. Shit, shit he said hunching down in his car praying no one saw him. Hey, that car over there a woman yelled. He peeled off in a hurry leaving tire marks in his tracks.

26

King in his crew was on the porch in a flash looking around, "who the fuck" king banged his hand against the door. Watching that strange car speeding off the seen. Let's go, "now" he yelled. the entourage rush back inside fearing he would flip out. Is this what the "fuck" I pay yawl for he questioned. I take one step to answer a fucking call, and no one notice a mother fucker in the yard? Huh, he was devastated. More so because he had no idea who it could have been, stupid mother fuckers. Was it that bitch" pasha he thought in his head. Shaking the thought, nah that bitch knows Imma kill her. I pay you worthless clowns for what? I could have almost got killed" you know what, all you mother fuckers get the fuck out. King one of his boys called out, he turned around slowly." what" bro I admit I was lacking, but you know I got your back. Since I believe you, plus you owned up you could stay. The rest of you clowns got about 30 seconds before my gun goes off. Nobody said nothing, they cut without another word. As soon as the crew got outside and inside the car a dude by the name of Rome said, so he thinks he somebody and he going to play me like I'm pussy. Nah I going to find this nigga low and flip the switch on his ass, just like he did on me. "bitch nigga" so yawl down with me he asked as he looked over his shoulders to the back. Hell yeah, that nigga broke another dude said laughing. I am sick of hearing that bear with me ass nigga. I got to eat, word they all agreed then they pulled off. Let's see who really could do em dirty. Times really changed Rome thought as he drove, his mind was running wild. I should kill "this nigga, he said to his self yet out loud. Who bro? he said who

29

what, nobody bro, he said realizing he had voiced his true feelings out loud. Bro do you think you can get away with killing him, his boy asked him. Rome chuckled without a response, boy straight up fool if he thought he was answering him, because if he did he would sell him out quick to the knocks. Nigga what you need to figure out is how niggas is about to eat, Rome said then turned the radio on.

CHAPTER 3

31

Nigga slow down dude said to his boy who was driving on the highway, but his boy didn't hear him cause of the music playing. He tapped his man, nigga stop the fucking car. The guys who name was Manny stopped the car a little, what the hell bro he said. You acting like the narcs is behind us or some shit, bro I think we just drove passed a "dead body" his man said with his eyes wide opened. Ha, ha-ha, nigga you must be high as shit Manny said. Nigga

32

back up" word to if I back up and it isn't no dead body I'm going to" shoot" you. Manny said in a serious tone, he began backing up. Stopping the car, he realized it was indeed a body. Oh shit" they both said in union, hell no! I am gone Manny the driver said. He began to drive away, bro what are you doing she looks alive. Mark if the bitch is or isn't I will not get charge for ether, Manny said. Nigga we can't just leave shorty, I got a fucking sister duke. now go back and we call for help. I swear if I get blame for this shit" I am going to body you mark. He

33

backed up and they both got out, marked went to lean over her and she grabbed his arm. Oh shit" he jerked away from her. Help me" help me, please. The duo looked at each other and figured taking her to the nearest hospital would best, there was no phone service. so, it was a waste of time trying to call anyone. Ok, ma what is your name? mark asked. She was whispering so low he leaned in closer, ma I can barely hear you. Man let's just get her in the car and let the fucking hospital deal with the bitch. Mark turned towards him and his eyes burned holes in

34

Manny. He decided the time wasn't now to address

Manny bitch tendency's, shorty needed help or she

was good as dead. He responded, man help me get

her in the car, before she dies out here. They lifted

her up gently and put her down in the back seat. But

mark decided to sit in the back with the girl, nigga

fuck is you doing bro Manny questioned with a

confused look on his face. Once again, he looked at

him square in the eyes, this time he spoke. If you

don't get shorty to the nearest hospital and fast theirs

going to be two admittances. Shocked Manny just

turned around shaking his head and pulled off, he whispered nigga tripping over this hoe. Reyna woke up and to her surprise she wasn't tied up or anything. Ah" she said she was in some serious pain but the room she was in was beautiful. "what the fuck" she shook her head looking around, one minute she was forced into some car and now she was waking up in a fucking huge house. But who's house was the questioned. She walked towards the windows and the view was breath taking, she was all kinds of confused. There were kids jumping in and out of a

36

pool, as if there wasn't a care in the world. Not one face of anyone outside was familiar, scratching her head. Somebody loves me she kind of chuckled, of course somebody loves you. A voice from behind her said and a female at that, she froze in her tracks. Excuse me she said without turning around, her heart was beating triple times. Candy knew what was going on. She knew Reyna all so well. she was trying to pretend she didn't know the voice. Ray I had to candy said, he would have killed me. you know it, it was now confirmed candy faked her

37

death. Rayna stood as still as a statue, while the tears dropped from her eyes. Ray please, forgive me candy begged walking up on her and grabbing her. Reyna just stirred out the window with and blank expression, she finally spoke why, just why she kept screaming. Do you have any fucking idea the pain you caused? Whap, she slapped candy, come on she began to swing again, candy backed up. Please don't hit me again, she knew the pain she caused her. Reyna was her heart, to see her in so much pain, because of her staging her death broke her heart in

38

two. Ray you have to understand please, sis she cried. He would have killed me, he really would of "killed me" who Reyna questioned. Low she asks laughing devilishly? Yea, she answered in a low voice, candy is you fucking kidding right now. No fucking way, your full of shit do you know that? What candy stood up and said in rage you have no fucking clue who my husband is bitch". Yea the fuck I do "bitch" they began fighting. someone heard them fighting and tried to break them up, Reyna tossed a vase crashing the wall just missing candy's head. The same fucking way you got me here, you trifling bitch" you better get me the fuck out of here. "now" candy couldn't believe what was going on. This is my life not yours, you never lived my life; and you have no clue she cried. Guess what "fuck it" he should have killed your trifling ass; do you have any damn idea someone killed Chica she yelled. Reyna was angry she wanted blood. At this point to tell her she was behind Chica murder would have cause so much more chaos she decided against it. Candy didn't say another word she got up and

40

walked out, what did she really expect a party. Yea I see what this is, do em dirty she yelled. It was so quiet in the house not a sound could be heard for at least an hour. Reyna laid on the bed crying so hard, until she heard the soft baby cries. Her heart broke in two she sat up, got off the bed and walked towards the door; was that baby low. She followed the sound until she reached the room the cries came from, it was. Her eyes got bold, her hand covered her mouth. She slowly approached candy, she looked at her and had to restrain herself from chocking that bitch".

Reyna backed peddled slowly still shaking her head.

Wait" ray candy pleaded no" I just got to get as far

away from you as possible. Reyna was really fucking

aggravated, ray please let us not do this again. Please

ray just fucking listen damn" light chuckles. Bitch"

you got two fucking minutes before I walk the dogs

on you, and trust this time won't be no getting me

off you. Candy didn't want to lose her sister, they

had been through so much, she loved her beyond

words. Sit with me ray, talk please, and do not drag

it. Ok, she breathed heavily, low used to beat me.

42

Ray just stirred at her while rolling her eyes at candy, when I say beat me. he used to black both my eyes. Raising her sleeves, she showed Reyna all the cigarette burns, it looked disgusting. What the hell Reyna shouted" candy cried turning around, she had all kinds of slashes from a razor on her back. He fucking did that to you, I am going to kill" that bastard. Reyna screamed so loud she made the baby cry, ooh auntie is sorry. She walked over to the crib and picked baby low up, she started singing a lullaby to him like she did at the hospital. and he went right

43

back to sleep. Even though she hated what candy

did, gosh she wanted to just beat her ass". over and

over but seeing what low did to her she tried to

understand, she really felt bad for not paying enough

attention to her friend. Reyna put little low back

down and walked over to her sister and hugged her.

Candy hugged her back, um not so fast missy Reyna

chuckled only way I will forgive you. Candy

finished is if we can watch money and violence,

hahaha you know it. Manny and mark finally

reached the hospital, mark rushed in. help, help

44

please a nurse rushed over. Yes, sir can I help you

she asked? I was driving and I saw a young female

on the road, ok where is she. She in the car, the nurse

yelled for assistance and they rushed out with a bed.

As they ran towards the car, Manny got out and

helped them get her out and on to the hospital bed.

Sir, do you know her name? no as I told you I was

driving and saw her laid out on the road, Mark

replied. So, is she going to be okay he asked. Nigga

lets go, Manny yelled she isn't our problem boy. The

nurses had rushed her in screaming for help, she

barely had a pulse. I'm going in with her! What, you don't even know that bitch" for all we know she deserved it. Mark kept it pushing and entered the hospital, when he got in he ran fast. To catch the room door, they took her into from closing, he didn't know why he stayed he just did. Sir, you cannot come in here one of the nurses yelled. The other nurse who originally attended him when he came noticed him, sir she said with a smile. Let us handle it, I will come out and update you, she said and winked. She was joyed that this young man who was no older than twenty-two saved this lady and even stayed behind. Mark shook his head and walked out. Manny was blowing up his phone, he kept sending his calls to voicemail.

Low pulled into a hotel off peters creek road he was tired as hell. He knew no one would be looking for him there, he got his key and proceeded to his room. He wanted to just die, the police kept calling his phone. He knew they was full of shit, so he brought a burner phone from town, he knew they would trace it. So, he would decide to play truth or dare with these assholes. He placed the long overdue phone call, officer Daniel's missing division. Um, yes hello this is Larry calling to see if there have been any leads on my son kidnapping. The officer began to stutter, he was trying to get another officer attention. so, they could trace his call. Hello, Larry barked. Yes, we do, we have been led to a Brooklyn apartment complex he said loud enough trying to get his partners attention. His partner was busy on the phone in his own world. He was heated. He had low

48

on the phone feeding him bullshit for ten minutes. So, why aren't you telling me you have my fucking son? Are you bitches" just eating fucking donuts he barked and ended the call.Low speeded down the highway, his mind was going crazy. He now knew kings hiding spot but where was his little man, he was filled with so much anger he lost focus and "boom" he had a head on collision with the car ahead of him. His head hit the stirring wheel. The car in front went tumbling over and hit another car, the highway was packed. A man got out his car to go check on low because he wasn't moving, others checked the two other cars that also collided. As the man had gotten closer to low car it blew up. "boom" the man was knocked back about twenty feet in the air. All you could hear where screams from everywhere. It was craziness all over, cars were blowing their horns trying to get around. One man yelled "shit" hope those cock suckers are dead, I have to get to my mom funeral. Are you fucking dumb one lady yelled? Maybe that's why your momma dead, because you're a jerk. She was heated, he ran towards her" wham he knocked her upside her head. Bitch if you ever in your life disrespect my dead mother I will "kill" you he said hitting her repeatedly. A group of guys ran and the began grabbing him off of her, one man yelled at him from a distance. Your ah "bitch" hitting on a woman. As he yanked away from the guys he began fixing his shirt and checking his hand. He yelled "suck my dick". All hell broke loose, the guy started walking his way without saying nothing. The crowd starting clearing out, as he got closer the guy got in fighting stance. Oh, so you want these hands to he asked? In one quick flash he just lost his life, the man pulled up on him and pulled out a forty. Blocker, block, blocker that man wasn't with the shit, once his body dropped, he stood directly over him and spit. He turned to the crowd "hey" somebody go in his phone call someone tell them his mother has company. No one moved. Everyone was lost for words, what a fucking day a lady said. The guy turned towards the crowd again, words of the wise don't ever tell someone to suck your dick unless you want to die.

You could hear the ambulance and police sirens coming. It was so many crashed cars, people were screaming because there were trapped in their cars. It wasn't enough ambulance to cover the seen, as the ambulance got out they were pointed in serval directions. Help, please help, my baby a lady screamed. The ambulance rushed over and was able to retrieve the baby boy, unfortunately not the other. it exploded, body parts and parts of the car went flying. The news reporter cookie caught it all, hello, yes this is cookie reporting to you live on I-85 what

53

we have here is one of the city's worst day in history. We have eight dead bodies from what started out as a car crash, then leading to a man physically assaulting a woman for talking about his dead mother. Following after that, quickly lead to his death, for telling a man who is sitting in that blue Bentley over there to suck his dick. Where trying to get towards the car that originally caused the accident. It is so badly destroyed from the explosion as you can see, I am hoping and praying for the driver. But from the looks of it, there doesn't seem to be any bodies found, the fire department is ripping

through what remains are left to the car. What a sad

day this is, thank you this is cookie from channel one

news. Greg back to you.

CHAPTER 4

Pasha and her beautiful daughter Mariah, sat in the back of their home. Life over the past few years had been amazing. Mariah bad memories were washed away, she had a normal life. Mommy, can we go to the mall she asked? Pasha looked at her princess, of course. Anything for you, Mariah screamed yes. Mommy I want a lot of dresses, shoes, and I also need my hair done. Pasha laughed. So, may I ask who you getting all dolled up for? Hum, nobody mommy I just like to always look good. Lol, so there isn't no one in particular at school, she asked. Mom, I am a queen. Yes, you are indeed, however for the past couple of weeks I have seen a change. No, well I do think this one person in my school is kind of cute. Hum, so what's his name her mother asked? Mariah looked at her mom, turned and began twirling her hair around in her hands. What's wrong honey she asked. Nothing, it's not a him it's a her, her mother was speechless. She cleared her throat, she was baffled. Here it was her daughter just turned twelve years old, and has a like for girls. Um, you like a girl honey she asked with her eyes wide. Yes, Mariah whispered, so tell me about this girl. What is her name and what is it that makes you truly believe you like her. As she began to answer her mom her mother phone began to ring. Pasha looked down, hold that thought I have to take this call.

She walked off the porch and into her house, it was rah meek. She hasn't seen him in years, after helping her get away from king. They spoke every few days though, hello sexy. Was sup he said. Why haven't I heard from you in almost three weeks. Listen pasha I have way too much shit going on, I will be there in a couple hours though. Omg, are you for real she screamed with full of joy. He laughed, yea I will. I can't wait she said, so you going to do that thang I like he asked. Oh yea, I'm going to suck that dick and jump up and down like I was jumping rope. He laughed, can't wait dick getting hard just thinking bout what that mouth does. Well, let me go and pipe down my wife. What? Are you fucking kidding she could not believe him? Look, yes, I will fuck my wife before I come to you. Did you fucking forget you are my side chick, I fuck you because I want to bitch" now get that mouth ready, so you can swallow these kids? Click line goes dead. Ugh, she screamed and tossed her phone against the wall. Who the fuck does he think he is she screamed, no I will not accept any more abuse from no man.

She walked back out on the porch to get her Newport's, she was in rage. She grabbed her Newport's and lit one, blowing the smoke out pasting back in forth. Mommy Mariah called out, not

61

now little girl. I don't want to be bothered she yelled. Whatever, rah must not be giving you no money she uttered. Walking away, what the fuck" you just said little girl. She had Mariah by the throat, oh so you smelling yourself huh, cause your dirty ass like girls now. Mariah was shocked, scared and could barely breath. She grabbed her mother's hand trying to get her hands from around her neck. Wapp, pasha began attacking her daughter, screaming all kinds of insulting words at her. Pasha lost control just that fast, she loved her daughter. Yet she hated her

62

because she was a rape baby, her cousins baby. She tried to love her whole heartedly, she thought the hate would eventually go away. It didn't! every time she looked at Mariah she would see kings face. Mariah began fighting her mother back.

Oh, so you want to grab on my hair? Pasha yelled, she put a beating from hell on her. poor Mariah was beaten to death. Once she realized Mariah wasn't moving nor swinging back, she stopped. Oh gosh, she kneeled down searching for a pulse. There wasn't one. No god, oh no god! What the fuck" have

I done. Mariah was dead. She pulled Mariah into her

arms, she screamed so loud. No one was there. She

couldn't move, she had broken her phone. She

couldn't call for help, she was about to go to jail for

murdering her only child. She got up and carried her

baby girl in the house. she took her upstairs and laid

her in her bed and tucked her in with her teddy bears.

She kissed her forehead, turned and walked out

closing the room door behind her.

Pasha reach the stairs and started screaming, the hallway mirrors shattered to pieces. What is wrong with me she yelled, god if I never needed you then, I need you now. She slowly walked down the stairs and entered her din, she grabbed her bottle of henny. She drank it straight from the bottle, she began talking to herself. Little bitch should have been talking shit. Look at you, now your dead. Dum as little bitch" she said with a grin. Never wanted kids anyway! She began to finish off the rest of her liquor, after clearing her throat she walked upstairs.

65

She went in her room and opened up her closet pulled out the safe, where she kept her gun stashed at. she pulled it out and looked at it, she kissed it and walked out the room towards her daughter's room. Just before she entered her daughters room she heard a car door slam, she froze in her tracks. Oh shit" rah she said. What the fuck" she ran back in her room and tossed the gun under Neath her bed.

Yo, rah called out. She came flying down the steps jumping in his arms. He hugged her, he put her down and noticed she was drunk. She smelled like she had been drinking all night. You drunk he asked? She played it off, you said you want to fill what that mouth does right. She dropped to her knees, ripping his belt off. She put his dick in her mouth and swallowed him hold. Fuck" oh shit girl. Yes, suck that dick bitch". He came within 60 seconds. Damn, he yelled after she swallowed them babies. He then proceeded pushing her to the floor move slut, and where is your daughter he asked? She turned and walked away, she stayed at a friend's house, she will

67

be back later though. Good he said now go pour me a drink, and suck this dick again. Ok, she poured his drink. She pulled off his boots and started pulling his pants off, he took the drink and swallowed it down. as she dropped back to her knees he pushed her back with his foot handing her his glass, another drink hoe. She slowly got up and walked over to get him another drink. This time she grabbed the bottle and brung it back. She poured his drink, sat the bottle on the floor. Now come suck this dick, oh and you aren't getting no dick. I wouldn't dare fuck you again hoe. She dropped down and started sucking his dick, he called her every slut, nasty bitches in the book. He was about to come, get off me bitch he stood over top of her and came all over her face. Once he was done, he got up and went upstairs. He yelled over his shoulders wake me up in an hour. She laid on the floor crying uncontrollably, ten minutes past she finally got up. She was tired, she walked up the stairs and checked on Mariah. She then proceeded into her room, rah was out like a light. She kissed his forehead and reached under her bed

69

and grabbed her gun. She looked at him, thoughts of

all the pain she had in her heart. No more pain, she

lifted the gun and pulled the trigger.

CHAPTER 5

Low didn't know what to do, the house he went to of kings was not where he had his son. He had steaked out there for two years. Every day, he was stressed

71

out to the max. Reyna, Chica had just vanished.

Honestly, he believed they were dead, he was on the

run for vanity murder. He was staying with a female

he met a year ago. He was getting money, he didn't

have a choice. He had to stay away from king spot

for a while, he didn't want to get caught. It has been

a whole year since he been over there. It was time to

go pay king a visit, it wouldn't be a nice one either.

He was going to walk right up to the door, knock or

kick that bitch" clean in. it was too much time gone

by and no trace of his little man. He had nightmares,

every night. Waking up heart beating fast, forehead sweating. Its time king pays. He had already killed kings whole crew; the Bronx was now the number one for triple homicides in New York city.

Hey, beautiful low said to his wife candy. She was sitting in her chair stirring out the window, without turning she threw her hand in the air. Low knew she was upset because he hadn't come home in 2 days. He began singing her favorite song, I did you wrong, you did me wrong. You take me back, she then turned towards him. She was silently crying, he grabbed her up and made her dance. She did, she was just glad he came home. I am so sorry, I should have called but my phone died baby girl.

For some odd reason she didn't fight with him, that spooked him. Surely, she would have thrown something at his direction or pulled away from him. Yet she didn't and that was very much different. He pulled her face up so they can be face to face. Do you forgive me he asked? She shook her head yes than walked away and sat back in the chair. Honey, is there something else bothering you he questioned? She finally spoke, Larry I'm pregnant. He looked at her and ran towards her, what? He was filled with joy, they had been trying for ten months. Hundreds of tests but each time they were all negative. He began rubbing her stomach, so you do know it is going to be a boy, right? She laughed slightly, it better not be. As mad as she was at him, nothing was ever strong enough to stop her from loving him. She knew through all the drama, he was a good man. She was lucky. He was pure and he was

baby momma free, she was his first and only wife, and first to give him his child. As he thought about those special moments, he became sick. How could she just leave me? He yelled, he got on his knees and started praying. Father, I know I don't pray often however, I really need you. I need you to bring my son back to me, I know I treated his mother wrong, I was stupid but I promise to raise my son up to be better. In the name I pray, amen.

He got up and walked over to the window, he stirred at the rain falling. He leaned against the window until he noticed a strange car parked. It was a four-door black Chevy with tinted windows. He moved out the window and started peeking, it looked like someone was inside. He tried to look inside but the tints were to dark, "fuck" he walked over to the nightstand a grab his rolled up blunt. As he lit it his phone rang, yeah hello, it was his man calling him to talk about a drop off. Where you at he asked the caller? Alright, bet I'm going to need you here like in a beat. Line goes dead. He walked over to the window, shit" the car was gone. How? Now he was tripping, he didn't hear the car go off nor pull off. He grabbed his phone and started dialing. Nigga hurry the fuck up! Don't ask no fucking questions, just get here. Click he ended the call. He started walking back in fourth, talking to his self. Who the fuck" was that. "boom" his door came flying in. oh shit" it was

78

too late; the guns were all pointing at him. Nah, he thought this isn't happening right now. Who was these mother fuckers, he didn't have beef with no crackers? So, he thought. They tied him up and repeatedly pistol whipped him. He passed out a few times, but they woke him up every time. Oh, no, tuff guy don't give up on us now. One of the white tall white man who looked rushing. He picked low head as he began to lose consciousness' again. Come on now the fun is just getting started. Low looked up, he was confused as to what was going on. Life really

79

just flipped its switch without any notice, he spit in the man face. Fuck you" you plain donut looking mother fucker. Then laughed wickedly, kill me" I don't have shit" I'm not afraid. The rushing guy was furious he went in to rage, you're going to die". He raised his hand and went to send a bullet straight threw his forehead. Stop" his boss said walking into the room, no; this spit bag spit in my face. Calm down, you will have your chance. Low looked up and was shocked to see who the man was. What the fuck" he shook his head, there was no way. After opening his eyes again to make sure his eyes weren't deceiving him. It was indeed the fucking doctor, that delivered his son. Oh, don't look so fucking surprised! You aren't nothing but the tissue I wipe my ass on. The doctor laughed. Ha,ha,ha I guess you really thought you would get away, with that disrespectful shit you said at the hospital. Right? Low turned his head and spit on the floor. He then turned back and spit on the doc feet. That sent the doc up in flames" you scum of earth piece of shit he yelled. Give me that gun, now" as he aimed his gun

81

towards low bullets started flying. Splashing one guy's head on the ground and another. Doc immediately ran for cover returning gun fire. Low laughed loudly, his men was late but on fucking time. He knew something was up, making that call was well worth it.

CHAPTER 6

So, what's the deal today Reyna asked candy? To be

honest candy really wasn't in the mood. She was

looking at Larry junior, seems like yesterday he was

born. Now he is running around calling her and going to daycare. He was saying daddy and that crushed her. He didn't even know him, yet he was screaming his name. it was days she just wanted to end the madness. Hello, Reyna said again because candy hadn't responded. Oh, my bad girl, I just got a lot on my mind right now candy said. Hum, like what Reyna questioned, we have been here for a while drama free. Isn't that why you left and staged your death, and kidnapped your own son? Candy looked at her with hate in her eyes. She done had

84

enough of Reyna bullshit, every chance she got she would throw it up in her face. Ok, bitch I've done had enough of this bullshit" yes I staged my "fucking" death. Yes, I had my son kidnapped, and had fucking Chica killed. You didn't live my fucking life Reyna! Wow, hold the fuck up" did you just say you had Chica killed? Yes, it was me ok! That bitch" had my fucking cousin in the hospital fighting for her life. Once I found out she was going to make it, here you go bringing that bitch in my life. I was plotting on that trifling hoe, the whole time. Nah, you can't be trusted, and I have to get away from you. I can't believe you, just when you think you know someone. Reyna was in shock, she began walking out the room. Ray, candy called out. She stopped and when she turned around her eyes was full of tears. What? she spoke barely over a whisper, she fucked your nigga, and had him killed while you were pregnant. Reyna stood there for a second and then began to speak all while wiping her tears. I forgave her candy, I forgave her. Sister for eternity, right? Hoes over bros. candy tears began to fall. she didn't want to tell her, yet her anger got the best of her. Reyna turned and walked out, she grabbed her purse and left. She refused to take anything, those years she didn't want to take with her. It was goodbye! Goodbye forever.

Reyna waited outside for her ride to the airport. As the car pulled up she turned and looked at the home she spent almost three years in. she watched candy in the window stirring. She got in the car and closed the door. It wasn't nothing left for her there and she can't no longer trust candy. She knows candy was her sister, yet so was Chica. Yea she had bad blood for Chica after what happened. But she forgave her, she cried so hard on her way to the airport. Suddenly her phone vibrated, she didn't even bother to answer. It began to vibrate again, hello she yelled. Hello, I apologize I am looking for Reyna. She looked at the phone with her face screwed up. Yes, this is she, may I ask who I am speaking with? yes, how are you

88

doing? My name is Sammy, you spoke with me a while ago. And before he could finish, she interrupted him. Oh, yes hi, I apologize I have so much going on. You're the guy who is going to help find my sister right? Yes, mama, so do you have any information on her she asked? Yes, I do actually, her name is Latrice. He paused for a second, hello is everything alright she asked noticing his silence. Um, yes excuse me. As I was saying, her name is Latrice and she lives in p.a if you have a pen I can give you a number as well. Wow, thank you.

89

However, I must say she was in the hospital for some time due to poison. What do you mean she questioned, someone tried to kill her? Yes, but she lived and was released after a few weeks. Omg, I'm getting on a flight now, I will be in New York in three hours. Ok, bye, she ended the call. She has been on the search to find her for years. That's all she ever wanted in life was to find her sister. Her dream was about to come true. She thought out loud, who the fuck" would try to end her life. Hurry the "hell" up she yelled at the driver. I have a flight to

90

catch. She wasn't trying to be there any longer, she had an address for her sister. and she wasn't going to waste another fucking" second on anything but finding her fucking sister. she was going straight to her home and reuniting with her sister. she had love for her friends, that she had known her whole life it seemed. there was no honesty, no loyalty, to many secrets. it was time for change, it was fucked up the ones in your corner was the ones who deceived you first. But finding her sister was all that's she ever wanted, nothing was about to get in her way of that.

91

she was just so sad because she was about to walk away from a sister, but she was about to gain her fleshing blood. one she knows in her hearts of hearts won't betray her. she felt so bad about Chica dyeing, and how she left her, her mind was running a mile a minute. she didn't know if her sister would welcome her with opened arms. she just closed her eyes and said a silent prayer, she just wished life could just go back to normal. she made it to the airport and realized it was time to face the big city, she sorts of dreaded it because there were to many bad

92

memories. Chica being killed, peaches also being killed in her face and in her arms. She lost her phone so she had no idea if low was ok, it was just too much going on. She has been gone from her home town for over two years. She didn't know what was in store for her but she would take it by storm. She wasn't about to run no more, so whatever god had in store for her she was willing to handle it. It was just that damn simple.

Chapter 7

Hey sweetie, what we going to do today king asked his sister Latrice? They had become very close once she had gotten out the hospital, she had no one. Low was gone. Without any trace that he ever even existed. King would ask her about him constantly, she couldn't answer him. He had all kinds of questions about who tried to kill" her. She didn't have any clue. Her life was going good until low showed up. She heard her brothers question, she just chose to ignore him. What she really wanted to know was where was the man she finally decided to love

94

was. How did the girl end up dead at her job, but she knew that after two years low being gone was forever? The females she helped, didn't do anything but make matters much more worse. She had decided she was out of work for too long. All she wanted was to put that life behind her and get back to work. Yes, her brother treated her like royalty, but she didn't like doing nothing. Bro, its time I go back to work I can't take this shit no more. I am being escorted everywhere like I am a I witness I'm done. She stated and got up, she walked in her closet and began taking out a two-piece blazer. Her boss already explained that she could always have her job back. Baby sister I am sorry if me protecting you is bothering you, all I want to do is protect you and keep you safe. Someone tried to kill you" I don't want to lose you, when you just got in my life. He walked over to her, you don't need to go back. Look, I am thankful I have you. Ok, I have to do this for me she said placing her hand on his shoulders. Now, what you can do for me is order me some grub. I am starved she said laughing, then she walked in the bathroom to shower and closed the door. Hey dee

she screamed opening the bathroom door, yes sis and

no tailing, I got this and she closed back the

bathroom door. King couldn't believe this shit, after

everything he did for her she just decided to run

back. Ungrateful ass! He had so much going on in

his life, not only did candy give him her ass to kiss.

She just straight up disappeared without a trace. He

paid the doctor two million dollars to stage her

death, have the baby kidnapped out the hospital.

Then she just up and changed her number,

97

everything. These damn sisters of his aren't shit, if they think that they can run in these damn streets alone with no protection. Than fuck it' he had other fucking" fish to fry. His whole team was damn near dead. He had no damn clue as to who was knocking them off, literally three at a time. He still hasn't found this bitch pasha, she got away with all his bank. What was he supposed to do if his man didn't give him some upfront bread to get back on his feet. He decided to say fuck" everybody! Family and all. If Latrice want do go back to work like a fucking" dummy, he would let her. He grabbed his coat and car keys and kindly bounced. He also left his phone, he didn't want to be reach. Latrice said fuck "him, well "fuck" her. That would be the last she heard from him. As Latrice got out the shower she slowly dried off, she was happy as ever. She started humming to herself, today was the day of a new beginning. As she wrapped her towel around her body she watched herself in the mirror, she was a slim beauty. Her hair was silky like a Brazilian, she opened the door and realized king wasn't in her room. She didn't pay it no mind she brushed it, thinking instead of ordering her food he went out to go get it. He always seemed to do it, he hated ordering thinking someone could be setting them up. She laughed to herself, he lucky he is my brother, he could have got this. She sat on her bed and lotion her body, she got up afterwards and gotten dressed. She put her ponytail in, wrapped it up in a tight bun. She noticed king was taking rather long and she proceeded to call him, as she called him she heard his phone ring, it was on her dresser. Damn it boy,

100

why would you forget you phone. Her thought

changed once she had gotten a knock on the door.

She yelled, about damn time. First you leave your

damn phone, now your keys. She swung opened the

door and it wasn't king, it was Reyna. What the

fuck" how did you find my crib she asked? Reyna

was fucking shocked, wait a damn minute. Why are

you at my damn sister house? How the fuck does

you know my sister? What? No honey I think you're

at the wrong house, because this her house belongs

to me. Now if you don't excuse me I have to get

101

back to work, oh yea the one you piece of shits came to. Bitches dies, I almost died, somebody tried to kill" me. Oh, what happen to your fucking" piece of shit brother she was going off. Reyna stood there with a blank expression. Oh, so you have nothing to say now right? Okay, before I beat your ass" I am going to kindly ask you again. May I please, please speak to the owner of the house. See, now I think you feel like you can talk to me any kind of way. First your bitch ass was being disrespectful at my job, but now I am off work and you at my door.

102

What is really good hoe? Girl, o girl you don't want this beating I fucking" promise. Reyna said meaning every word. Latrice decided against it, Fuck it, who is your sister? Ok, thank you" my sister name is Latrice. Ha Latrice laughed in her face, bitch please" I'm her and you aren't my damn sister now beat it hoe. Latrice went to slam the door in her face, Reyna put her foot in the door to stop it from closing. "bitch" are you crazy? She opened her door wide, look I don't know what fucking kind of game you're playing. But I swear you have ah bout two minutes

103

before I shoot you. Ok, what I am about to say may seem crazy but it's not a joke. Girl, on everything you have a couple of seconds. Look we have the same mom Reyna said, mom gave me up when I was first born. Latrice stepped back, she shook her head no your lying. I swear to you! She reached in her pocket and pulled out a baby picture, she handed to Latrice. She covered her mouth, she couldn't fucking believe it. It was the same exact one she had. She lifted her head up and stirred at Reyna, so what is your name than? Its Reyna! The tears came out of both of their eyes. How, why, they both had so many questions. Come in Latrice finally said, for them it was like a dream come true. They were sisters, they had already been together under crazy circumstances and didn't even know it. They laughed and joked and cried all at the same time. Until Latrice seen hours had passed in her brother never came back with her food. She said where the hell is this dame man at out loud. Who Reyna asked? Oh, I'm sorry, I have a brother. He left to go get me something to eat, I think he didn't come back on purpose because he doesn't want me working back at my job. Ever since that girl died, I got poisoned. With everything they talked about Reyna never asked her about Chica getting killed at her job. She was just so happy that she found her sister, she never even asked. Well, you cannot blame him he only wants to protected you. Shit I wish I had a brother to protect me she said. Latrice grabbed her hand, look we are sisters and he is my brother so that makes you his sister to. Reyna smiled, you think so? Of course. I cannot wait till he gets back so the two of you can meet. I love you sis, it feels like we have been sisters our whole life.

Reyna smiled it felt good to hear those words. So,

lets finish talking, what happen at the hotel that night

you got poisoned? Look, sis one minute I was called

to do an extra shift, next minute I was on the floor

dyeing. all I really can remember was I had just hung

up from talking to low, then my bossed called. I

walked to the back to get my drink out the fridge, by

the time I made it to the front I was hit with some

sharp pains. I don't really remember anything else, I

was in the hospital for too damn long. I heard

107

someone got killed in your room, honestly, I thought it was you. I told them some girl came for you and after that I couldn't give any more details. So, they told me low was there for two days, but when I woke up he was nowhere to be found. Latrice became sad, and Reyna knew why. Did you love him she asked boldly? Latrice looked her in the face, yes. Why did he just leave me? What did I do? All I tried to do was help him, he just used me. She became so emotional, it was too much for Reyna. She grabbed her sister, it will be ok sis. I promise, sometimes men

108

come for a short period to prepare us for another. Reyna tried to soothe her the best way she could, she knew that eventually she would have to tell her the truth, but now wasn't the time. So, tell me about this brother of yours. Latrice giggled a little bit, you mean our brother. Don't go getting any crazy ideas, because he is your brother to. Giggling Reyna said sis I know, so what's his name? is he a cute she asked with her eye brows raised. Yup, so tell your friends he is off limits. Shut up, Reyna said playfully hitting her with a pillow. His name is dee, hum ok.

109

Well that's his real name, his street name is king though. What? Reyna said, his street name is king? Please tell me king isn't his name she asked standing up? Is he from the Bronx? Sis, your making me fucking nervous now. Latrice said now standing up. Yea, he is. What's this all about. Oh, my fucking goodness, I have to get out of here. Reyna was fucking baffled, Ray what is wrong? She paused because no one calls her that, besides peaches and candy her whole life. Look, what I'm about to tell you is about to rock you to sleep. I'm not really sure how you're going to handle it, but this here isn't an

easy pill to digest. King has another sister; her name

is candy. She was my best friend, and the nigga low

your so in love with. Your brother hates him and

helped his sister candy fake her death and they

kidnapped the baby from the hospital. What are you

saying? Latrice was more confused now then she

ever was, wait a minute she said. Ok, let me get this

straight. My brother has a sister named candy, he

helped her fake her death, and kidnapped a baby

from the hospital. Yes, but who fucking baby did he

kidnap? Candy had a baby bye low, that's her husband. Low and candy had problems, and she didn't want king in jail for killing him. So, they paid the doctor a huge lump so of money to get of New York. What? No, you're lying! Why the hell would I "fucking" lie. Reyna barked. Why don't you ask him your damn self! You know what else, low and I accidently ended up at your job because someone tried to kill us. So, we decided to go lay low for a while, somebody killed low side bitch. They framed low, now the police are looking for low for her murder. I had no idea about any of this shit! Until the police showed up at the hotel, looking for low. We had no idea how they found him, but I guess you was down with it. Latrice had to laugh, you simple minded bitch! That isn't my fucking style, I am not a rat. How can one sit here in judge one she doesn't even know? I wish you never came knocking on my door, who is to say you're telling the truth anyway. Get out! Now! Wow, I guess you are as sneaky as that brother of yours. You, your brother and candy were all down with it. Latrice lung at Reyna they tore that house up, it was not a sole to stop them.

Truth be told Reyna was tarring that ass up, she had

to put an end to this shit. She sat on top of poor

Latrice, look little girl you can't rock with these

hands. mi going to warn you, once I get off of you. I

will proceed towards the door, and if you try to

attack me, I will beat your ass till you beg me to

stop. She used Latrice as a crutch to get up. Fuck

you" Latrice yelled at Reyna she was leaving and she

wouldn't return. She asked before she walked out

that door, so you chose to rock with king? She said

114

because once I walk, I will never return. Latrice started crying hard, this was too much for her to handle all at once. Who side was she about to choose? Is Reyna telling the truth? Was she really there looking to reunite with her, or was this a set up to lock up her brother for kidnapping. and all that other shit. It was like Reyna could read her mind, she walked over to her sister and hugged her. She bawled so hard in her arms, and Reyna tears also started to fall. She didn't want to leave her sister life, however life just jumped up by ten times, she now

115

had to ask herself could she even trust Latrice now with the truth. They both had trust issues, Reyna slowly released Latrice and lifted her chin up to look at her. Look baby sister, I have loved you whole hearted even without ever meeting you. I would never ever intend to hurt you. Ever! I have wanted to find you my whole life. My coming here was never the intention to hurt my fleshing blood. I swear, this was just a coincidence. Latrice walked towards the coach and sat down, yea, one big one. Now do you want to try this again? Yes, I want to know is low

116

really that bad that his wife staged her death and had her own baby kidnapped? Honestly, I cannot answer that. To me he was just and average man with jealousy issues. To her she says he is a monster, the scary ones you see in movies, Reyna said. Do you believe her she questioned? Truthfully, low has a lot of issues. however, I wouldn't say he is that bad. Little sister I don't trust anybody anymore, candy was my best friend. She staged her death after another one of our friends got shot dead and died in my arms, a few hours prior. The girl that came to the

117

hotel, attacked me at the same damn time, because she blamed me for her getting killed. I almost got blown up leaving the hospital with low. What the hell? What do you mean almost got blown away? Well, as me and low was leaving the hospital, I received a call from some guy demanding I put low on. After low ended the call, we were about to get in the car it blows the fuck up. Omg, Latrice screamed hugging her. Sis I am so sorry, all of this happened to you. Nah life took a turn for the worse, it's so scary. I don't have a clue as to what is going on any more. One minute were the do em dirty crew and the next were getting done fucking dirty. Now, the girl you sent up to my hotel that night someone tried to kill you. Yea, well she was like a sister to me to. Reyna started to tear up, she was the one killed that night. Covering her mouth Latrice couldn't understand what type of shit her sister was into. Being around her may not seem to be in her best interest. Wait, wait a minute, did you kill her she asked Reyna? No, soon as you called I unlocked the door, and was about to take a shower. Someone came in as I went to run the shower, I heard the door close and I thought it was her. I began to tell her come in the bathroom, but as I turned around it was a female pointing a gun at me. Oh, hell to the no! how the fuck did the bitch get past me and into your room she thought out loud. Oh, shit I remembered a female and a guy came and got a room prior. I mean I don't know if they had anything to do with it, but that was the only people I can remember coming around the same time. Ok, okay there was two females and a baby that came two hours earlier. Wait, you said baby? Yes, why Latrice asked? Is there any way you can access the camera's? Ray you do know that was two years, ago right? Damn, right. No wait a second, no one has access to that lock box but me. However, I have the tapes in my room, I had them after I gotten released from the hospital. I saw the bitch that tried to kill me but I couldn't recognize her. Hold tight Ray, let me get them out my closet. Reyna cannot believe this is happening. Isn't funny how life work, after all these years and in a fucked-up situation she finds her sister. I'm back, Latrice flopped on the coach and started looking through the surveillance

CDs of that day. Got it! Reyna was so anxious to see

that shit, ok she was about to fast forward it. Wait,

what the fuck? Pause it right there, Reyna had gotten

up and started walking back and forth. What she saw

was even more crazier than she thought. What's

wrong Ray? You wouldn't know even if I told you

sis, well still what is it she questioned? Look, you

see the two girls with the baby? Yea, well that's

candy and lows son. Oh, damn what the hell is going

on? That girl has been here three days prior with

122

another man. Another man Reyna asked? sis I said yes, actually the man walking up right now as they walk away from the desk. Yo, this has to be a joke right she said to her outside voice. That is fucking rah meek and Lg, this is too much for me. what do they have to do with this sis? Please give me a second and what she saw was enough to make her sick, pasha was with rah. She is the bitch who was supposed to have him robbed. This shit is beyond sickening, candy was involved in this whole set up. I am going to do this bitch dirty. Fuck this bitch, as she kept watching the tape she sees that there all involved. they knew blowing up the car would scare low, straight to the highway and he would go to the nearest hotel. Do em dirty huh, a few moments she watches the girl leaves out the room and onto her floor. Candy, rah meek and Lg all leaves and once they left you went to the back and that's how your drink got poison poured in it. Reyna kept watching all the way until the Chica came to her room, she saw herself leaving the room and all the falling to the floor. No, omg she is alive. Oh, my goodness, it

124

wasn't her who died, she's alive. Sis what are you talking about? She was so confused, my sister she's is alive. She killed that bitch she cried with tears of joy.

CHAPTER 8

Danny was so cracked out, he had no knowledge of anything. He had been on the run for two years, in the low eastside. He was fucking all kinds of men for a hit of crack. His lover put him onto it, he led him to believe it would cure his pain. Come on Danny his lover said, it's not as bad as you think. Watch me, he hit the pipe and it sent him on a mission. He was floating, please try it. You will see, it will have you floating like your in heaven. Danny watched how his partner gloated and decided to try it. Ok, let me try it. Just once though, he said as he hit the pipe he seems to feel so good. He wondered why he ain't been try it. He started swinging around any floating just like his partner. His partner new exactly what he was doing, he would pimp him like a crack head. All kinds of men would fuck on him, even three some's. Danny couldn't even tell them to stop, he didn't know how. One minute he would be smoking then the next he would be getting fucked, roughly in all kinds of positions. Before he could even scream from all the pain, someone would be passing the pipe to him. He would then forget all the pain, then someone else was up next. They would video him getting fucked doggy style and sucking another's man dick. His partner enjoyed watching, he would have dogged him afterwards. You expect me to fuck you" after you just let these men have their way with you for crack you fucking crack baby. Danny didn't know they made him the laughing stock, he was just the go to guy. An easy fuck. His partner was getting all the money, he was just keeping him high poor

Danny. Shit, even he was fucking women and eating they pussy. Some women thought his dick was the bomb, he made some good love to the woman. His partner even busted his head open, so you really like woman huh? Why are you fucking them so good? Danny was always high, he didn't know if he was fucking a man or women. Now, his partner was gone for days, he hasn't been outside in a year. He had grown so much facial hairs; his body was damaged goods. He totally forgotten he even killed a cop. He needed air, food, the water was so dirty. His lover left and never returned and wouldn't. his lover was released from prison and it was over for poor Danny. He got up and almost fail, he was determined to go outside. As he got downstairs, his legs grew weaker but he made it to the door and made out the entrance. As soon as the sun light hit his face he buckled, someone noticed him on the floor and ran over. Excuse me sir, are you okay, a man asked? The light was to bright, hello sir, do you need help? Danny tried getting up, he tried using his hands to block the sun. the man figured he needed help, he stunk so

130

bad, and was so skinny he looked half dead. The guy

called the ambulance. Sir, I called help, they will be

here shortly. At this point Danny didn't have a clue

he was soon going to jail. For the murder of a cop,

once they realized who he was. Sir, I need a hit, I

need food, you can fuck me' I promise you won't

regret it. Sir, help is on the way. This man felt bad

for him, whoever did this to you needs to burn in

hell" he said out loud. As he looked harder at Danny,

he seemed familiar. He looked a little closer than

shook his head, he pulled out his phone to check the

131

wanted list. It was indeed the man wanted for killing that cop, shit. He said out loud, come here, I got you. He knew killing a cop was wrong. But as many innocent black people cops killed, a few needed carma. He was grateful the ambulance didn't come yet; his son was a doctor. He would save this black man, he helped Danny stand up. Come on brother I got you, Danny didn't care all he wanted was a hit. This man knew helping Danny was about to be hell, but saving a life was better than losing a life. He knew for sure that if he was identified prison was up

132

next, but they would have had him killed. He looked

both ways and quickly got Danny into his car, and

drove off to his son house. Danny kept making all

kinds of noises in the back, the unknown man felt so

bad for him. Once he got him back to heatlh he

would find out if he had family, then reach out and

try to find them.

Chapter 9

Officer Mitchell's watched her son running around without a care in the world. He had gotten so big, he looked just like his father. She was comfortable in her new home, she had to move after the attempt to kill" her and her son. She couldn't believe that the brother of the guy who took her husband's life had the nerve to try in assonate them, she was a damn cop. However, after making that attempt he was killed. He, however did get into her home, and stake out inside for a few days. His mistake was, her home was full of hidden cameras. Inside and outside, he

134

thought he was good when he reset the outside ones. Dummy, if he knew better, he surly would have done better. She was a "fucking" cop. His brother had gotten away with killing, her husband. She be damned if they killed her to, she had camera's in her closets, her bathroom, and kitchen. All she had to do was check from her phone. One day she went to visit her family, she stayed for a few days. She decided to just check on her home, she sees a man in her house rumbling threw her shit. Then another in her closet, oh, no she said allowed to no one in particular. These mutha fuckers is about to pay, at first, she thought it was just some dummies trying to rob the crib. When she realized they weren't trying to, she knew it was serious. Instead of alarming her family, she asked if they could watch the baby. Of course, they did, so, she got in her car and drove home. She watched for hours, they made shit to eat, they even smoked. She didn't call none of her fellow officers, this was personal. As she pulled up to her home in Bickerton, she parked and sat in her car for a second to see their movement. As on point their positions changed, one headed to the closet and one under the bed. She slowly existed her car, she acted as normal as possible however, her heart was in overtime. She slowly entered her home, she pretended to be on the phone, she was really watching them. She dropped her bags, she proceeds up the stairs and entered her room. Her heart was beating uncontrollable, she pulled out her gun opened her room door. She watched as Lg began to lift his gun inside the closet, the door to the closet was still closed. She lifted up her gun, she squeezed until there wasn't no more bullets. Lg, body jerked and jerked until he came crashing out the closet. His boy laid there in shocked, his eyes were wide opened. He prayed he could make it out, Lg was faced towards him. He turned the opposite way, it hurt him bad. It was like he was screaming for help threw his eyes. What he didn't know was he was next, she reloaded her gun. He could hear her, instead of instantly killing him. She made him suffer, she laid on the bed for twenty minutes. At this point he had already died in his mind, he figured because she wasn't moving she was a sleep. He tried to move but she felt him, she sat up and pointed the gun and emptied it. He died instantly. She got up and pulled him from under the bed, and laid him next to his friend. She looked at them both, reloaded her gun again and shot them both in the head. She than picked her phone up and called the law. You scum bags came into my home trying to kill me, she kept yelling and shot at them again. She picked up some rum and got drunk, the police were there in a flash. She said they tried to rob me, so I killed them. When they got up stirs they saw it was an over kill, it was planned out. They saw the

holes in the bed and in the closet, they knew

something was terribly wrong. She showed them her

badge, they investigated and found out it was true.

Once the sergeant, got there and they realized the

over kill. They started asking all kinds of questions.

Officer Mitchell's do you know the suspects? No, sir

she responded. Where were the suspects when you

entered your home? Sir, one was in the closet. Ok,

the other, well, he was under Neath my bed sir, so

the sergeant walked towards the closet and closed it.

He looked at the officer, then at officer Mitchell's. So, by the looks of it, you shot into the closet, am I mistaking he asked? No sir, she answered truthfully, now I see the other gun shots that killed the other gentleman, was from on top of the bed correct? Yes sir, she again answered. So, you didn't seem like you were in danger to me he said. Sir, they would have "killed" me if I didn't "kill" them first. They are intruders she screamed, why are you acting like I planned this. I am the victim here, she yelled. Question? How did you know these intruders were in your home? She paused before she spoke, she wished her friends would have come to the seen. Of course, not though, it was some fucking rookies. Sir, no officer, answer the question he barked. I have surveillance connected threw my home, it alerts me to my phone if someone breaks into my home. Ok, so you see theses intruders in your home? Yes, so, why didn't you call the law enforcement instead of handling matters yourself he asked, with a raised eyebrow. Again, do you have any idea who these men are? No, I said got damn it! Now, get out my house. Excuse me, the sergeant said. Cuff her and take her in, I believe this was premeditated. What? Are you bullshitting me right now? Call my fucking lawyer, now! We will see you down at the station, the officer cuffed her, and took her handcuffed out of her home. She thought about how much life was different, her parents raised her son, for his first year due to her in the mental hospital. She moved out in P.A closer to her parents, she left the force and just became a mom, a widow. Only if times could rewind

143

back, she would have made sure her husband had on

his vest.

CHAPTER 10

Low couldn't fucking understand after two years, still no evidence of his son where about. He had to sneak out of his car after his accident. Then he was still on the run for a murder he didn't commit. Then the doctor from the hospital, tried to "kill" him. His luck for 2018 was fucking horrific, he killed" kings whole damn crew. Well, it was about two of them left, not including kings "bitch ass" they were in hiding. He knew sooner or later they would surface, and when they did he would be right there. You can only hide and be running for so long. He knew king

146

needed money, was no money, like New York

money. That's for certain, he was patiently waiting.

He just gotten word kings grandmother was in town,

since yesterday and king was on his way in town.

King still has no idea, he knows he was the

kidnapper. He was going to pretend he needed work,

act normal, then kill him once he told him were his

son was. Low had his mind made up, ether way he

was "killing" king period. Him and all his

nightmares, hot sweats, cold shower days were over.

It was time to end all the madness. He doesn't

147

believe in killing the elderly, but the fact that he

kidnapped his son, things were off limit. It just times

you have to make a statement. To many people

believed (not me) wrong. It can be anybody! Today

king would learn, right kid, wrong parent, he will

pay. Low decided to go shower. He had a long day

ahead of him, he turns on his system and plays one

of his favorite songs. (forever) by cardi b. beefing

with him will indeed be forever, until someone is

dead. He didn't believe in beefing, it causes to many

issue's. to much thought, so if it isn't about creating

a better life, you had to go. Problems solver was his

name. right as he was about to get in the shower he

got a call. Yea, bro what im about to tell you is going

to have you fuck the town up. His boy by the name

of JoJo said, shoot low replied. Ok, remember the

kids that used to hustle for king? Yea, well

something must have popped off and he came

looking for you. Fuck do you mean? Bro, your going

to want to hear this. Nigga ether you tell me or bring

the nigga to me, simple. Ight, the little nigga said

king and candy are sisters and brothers. he helped

her fake her death, and kidnap your little man. Low

face turns beat red and he brown skin. Nigga, what

the "fuck" you just say. Bro, I'm not joking! Where

this "bitch" nigga at? he sitting right here he

answered, on my way! Ight, and keep that nigga

there. Heard! The little nigga was shitting bricks,

what he say bro, the little nigga asked? Nothing, he

on his way. You think he going to kill me? I can't

speak for that man boy! Low, said fuck showering,

he threw on some sweats and bounced. He was about

to "kill" everything and anything moving. He was

150

bugging, how the hell, was they brother and sister he thought. He sped down the highway, he was more careful though, he didn't want to crash again. This "bitch" and her brother is dead! I put that on everything he said banging on the dash board.

CHAPTER 11

The man had gotten Danny to his son's home, he

was tripping and going crazy he wanted a hit bad.

They man fed him and was bathing him at the same

time. It didn't matter to him, that he was naked.

Danny just stunk really bad, his son was on his way.

He also previously was in the medical field, so he

cleaned Danny up and gave him an Iv so his body

could get the fluids he needed and some medicine to

make him rest. He needed some rest so he could be able to function, he didn't want the drugs to send him into shock. Danny fail to sleep quickly, he would wake up feeling much better. His son entered his home. Pops you hear, his son yelled. His father came downstairs, yea son I am. They hugged, so what's the deal with this dude his son asked? Well son, he is the young boy who killed the cop, two years ago. His son looked shocked, wow! So, how convenient he said and laughed. Man, as I was leaving this broad house he chuckled. Dad, you still fucking these young chicks? He asked and laughed, man pops done been just getting head that's all. What? Ok, anyhow I saw him cramped over, and I saw somebody had gotten him strung out. I called the paramedic's, then I looked a little closer and realized who he was. Nobody deserves to die, however these cops done killed to many of our peoples. They want him they will have to find him. He needs help, so were going to do so. Ok, I'm good with that, but once we get him back healthy than what? He asked his father, those two were best

155

friends. Once his father had gotten clean, because he was hooked on drugs bad. He had come back for him, he went looking for his daughter Latrice as well. Somehow, she wasn't able to be found, so whenever they did find each other he would explain his lifestyle. Hoping she would understand and give him a fresh start. He was doing great. Well son, when that time comes, we will go from there. He is sleeping now, so LET'S grab some drinks and play a game of chest his dad said. Chica woke up from a much needed nap, she looked up and saw her knight

156

and shinning armor, two years ago when she had to kill a much needed memory and escape from the hospital, she passed out on the highway. he stopped and took her to the nearest hospital, he saved her life. she woke up to him playing in her hair, she had no idea to where she was at, who was this man. she began screaming, she had visions of her still in prison. she had a horrible prison stay, she looked around and saw the hospital. she thought back to when she was in Albion correctional facility. she was at work in the law library, they called her to the chapel. she knew something bad happen, she could feel it. they told her that her sister had passed away. she freaked out real, really bad. she began screaming so loud, she fails to the floor. why? why? lord did you take her, why not me? i am the one who deserves to die! she was the good one, they tried to calm her down. get off of me, get the fuck off of me, she said hitting a female officer. they restrained her, please, please, we are so sorry for your lost. but if you don't come down, unfortunately we will have to put you in keep lock. we really don't want to, we know what you are going through. we can have

someone come talk to you if you would like? she

screamed fuck you bitch" and spit in the officer face,

"i will kill you" that's when the decided she has way

more issues. they took her straight to mental health.

and as they thought this girl, was suffering from way

TOO much depression. she also was diagnosed with

bipolar disorder. she should have been getting help.

the nurses began rushing in the room, because mark

had pushed the button. they had come in to calm her

down, she thought she was still in jail. I want to go

159

home, please, help me. mark stirred at her, she was

so beautiful. he wasn't going to leave her. he stayed

day in and day out for two weeks. she asked him

who are you? are you trying to kill me? he kindly

explained to her how he found her on a highway. all

he wanted was to make sure she was ok. she couldn't

believe she found someone so sweet, she smiled at

him. good morning sexy! he turned around and

walked up to her, good morning sweetheart. I made

you breakfast, hum, what did I do to deserve

breakfast, she asked playfully? what man wouldn't

make a woman who is smart, beautiful, strong, and

oh, so sexy breakfast. she laughed, shut up and threw

a fake punch at him. Those too had gotten a bond so

strong that no one could break. She had really turn

her life over because of him. She wasn't this

gangster girl no more, she had become Chantel,

Chica was gone. she was pregnant with her first

child, marks first child. Her in mark just up and

disappeared. like they were the only people who

exists, life was good for them. She was glad he came

into her life, he brought her a beautiful home. It

161

wasn't too big and it wasn't too small, however, it did have a back yard with pick it fence. Four bedrooms with chandelier's hanging thru out house, wall to wall carpet, an upstairs and downstairs. Chica had so many thoughts going on in her mind, no matter how far she traveled. she always thought of Reyna and how peaches were killed, and how candy died giving birth. She had so many unanswered questions, she shook the thought off. She ate her breakfast and decided she would go see a movie, the black panther. As Chica was getting out the shower her phone rung, it was unknown. Usably, she would have thought suspicious but she didn't have any reason to. Hello, she answered. Um, yes, I am calling to speak to Chantel Moore. She looked at the phone strange, then she spoke, yes this is she, may I ask who is calling? First, my name is Latrice and I'm your sister, she said flat out. Chica eyes grew wide as day, after all these years. she finally contacted her, wow! So how are you she asked? I am good, so you don't sound surprise to hear from me. Well, honestly, I've waited a very long time. Truth be told,

163

I have a lot of questions that I need answers to. Ok, Latrice responded so how about lunch this afternoon? I am in your town, can you meet me a Simpson's restaurant on the ave? yea, she responded. Great, how about in an hour Chica said. Sounds good, see you soon. They ended the call. After, ending the call, she looked at her phone. How the hell did she get my number, she asked herself. Baby, she called out to mark. He walked in the room, was good my sunshine. You are not going to believe this, she said. What? Did something happen he

164

questioned, yea babe. Now, remember I explained to you how my dad has another child. Yea, ok, why she just called my phone. What do you mean she just called your phone? Baby I swear, we have plans to meet in the town in an hour for lunch. So, how did she get your number they both said in unison? Right, my point exactly she said. Well, you're not going alone! It could turn out bad, you don't need no stress. You pregnant with my child, she smiled ok baby. She headed towards the bathroom, then turned around, make sure you look good. Heard, mark said,

165

you want her to look at you man huh he said

laughing. Be out in a second, ight ma I'm going get

ready as well.

CHAPTER 12

Phone ring. Hello, yea. Nigga I'm pulling up right now low said, you still got that lil nigga there he asked? Yea, he still here, nigga scared straight. Isn't no need and being scared now, I'm still going to kill this mother "fucker" open the door I'm getting out now. Click, he ended the call. He looked at the little dude and felt bad, he knew it wasn't nothing he could do. This was some serious shit, he didn't understand why he was about to die. Rule number one never switch sides, no matter what. Rule number two if your beefing with your, opponent ether handle it or push it forward. There is no in between, never tell. Street niggas keep it street. Low walked in and the little dude sat up, he put on the straight face hoping to score points. Wapp, low bitched slapped

168

him. What the "fuck" the little nigga said. Nah, nigga! You helped this "bitch" and her "bitch" ass brother kidnaps my "fucking" son. Low pulled out his heat, and clapped him once in the leg. Ugh, he screamed man please, nah mother fucker where is that "bitch" with my son he asked? The young man was on the floor rolling around screaming. "shut" your "bitch ass". So, what happen that you over telling, huh low asked as he shot him in the other leg. He screamed even louder, what you screaming for "pussy" he asked laughing. I hate snatch back

169

mother "fuckers" like you. He calmed his self-down, listen to me and listen well. I'm only asking you one time, think really good before you answer. Cause your family life depends on it. Now, where the "fuck" is my son he asked and raised his gun directly at his head. They are in Santa Maria, he quickly answered. Low, knew shorty was telling the truth, he looked at him and put his gun by his side. Get the fuck out! I don't care if you dye walking out, but you have about sixty seconds. Or I'm going to put a bullet in your head. Low, homeboy knew shorty

170

wasn't able to get up, he grabs shorty up and took

him outside and called the ambulance. Low didn't

stop him because he was only about twenty years

old. However, he hopes shorty learn from this, who

raise these kids he said to his self. He lit up his weed

and sat down. He was about to catch a flight out.

Chapter 13

Candy sat there as Reyna pulled off, she knew this time she has lost Reyna for good. She knew once she found out she had evolvements with Chica being killed, it would have put a huge damper in the relationship. Why couldn't she just leave this shit buried she cried. She wanted to run outside before she left, but she knew it was only going to cause an epic failure. As the car pulled off she went to call Reyna, but her phone started ringing. She hustled fast, she prayed it was Reyna. Who the hell, she didn't know the number. She wasn't about to pick that shit up, she was tired of bill collectors calling

her damn phone. Plus, she wasn't in the mood, she

was stressed. The caller called back, yes, hello she

barked into the phone. How you just disappeared

after everything king questioned her, answer me. She

was shocked, she responded how? How, what? I got

your number, after I save you from this bastard. She

started to speak, I was scared. Scared of what sister, I

paid bread for everything! He screamed. I am your

brother, if I can help you stage your death, what's

next huh he asked. You going to try it again. Oh, you

174

still have that do em dirty mentality huh. Well pack up! I am going to show you do em dirty. Click. What the fuck, she yelled looked at the phone. She was about to clear it, she didn't know what was to come. She had to get baby low and go, king was really a nut job, that she should have fixed a long time ago. She heads to little Larry junior room to check on him. As she walked in his she sees he was sleeping on the floor. She smiled, the picked him up and put him in his bed. Aww, mama baby can't hang she said as she put cover over him kissing his forehead.

She turned on the nightlight and walked out and closed the door. She went a poured herself a drink, if the bastard comes near me and my child. I'm going to "kill" him she said out loud while finishing her drink. She got in her bed and grabbed a book, and started reading. Then she heard a noise, she jumped up, she ran in lows room with her gun in hand. He was still sleeping, she closed his room door back. it was the dog, he knocked over the garbage can. Girl, she said laughing out loud you need to relax. She went back to bed, this time she passed out. Then five minutes later, it was another noise. She lifted her head then realized it was the dog. Had she had gotten up she would have seen, low and his crew taking her son. Their son! As bad as he wanted to "kill" her he used his brains, my son is going to need her one day. But not today, he got his son. He walked out the door with his son still sound asleep. They walked to the car where his driver waited and got in and pulled off. He looked at his little junior who was tossing and turning. He positions his self, so his boy was more comfortable. He kissed his forehead and whispered,

177

Daddy got you! I love you. Candy would now see how it feels to lose the only thing that matters. Candy got up after a long goodnight sleep, she sat there looking at the time, little Larry didn't come waking her up. Lord, what is this boy getting into she laughed. As she went in his room she realized not only was he not in his bed, his bed was made. It had a note on it, what the "fuck" she grabbed at the letter in a hurry. She was hoping it wasn't from king

Dear bighead

I know we had our problems, I will not deny that. Yes, I've cheated, was it fair to you? No! we fought psychically yes, lets be honest though. How many times have you punched me in the face? Attacking me, my family, in the street. Pulling my hair, scratching me in my face, and breaking everything, I owned? Was that fair? No! I know you don't like taking your medicine, but you have no choice at this point. Now, the only options you have now are to number one ether turn your self in, for faking your death and having our child kidnapped from the

179

hospital. She didn't even want to read no more, she just balled up and cried. Why? Why, god. What am I going to do know? she cried, she picked up the letter and began finish reading it. Now, since I know you don't want to go to prison, and even though I am beyond pist. I don't want my wife in their ether, so turn in your "bitch ass" brother. For also, framing me for murder. I don't really care about nothing else, I don't care if he is your brother either. That is also funny, your never even told me. You're a dum "bitch" so what that being said, I didn't do nothing

180

that deep, for you to take my son. Staging your death, staging my son to be kidnapped. You got twenty-four hours to turn that "bitch" nigga in anonymously, or I will turn you in. nooo, she screamed.

Chapter 13

Chica and her man, parked outside the restaurant

fifth teen minutes early. They wanted to make sure

there wasn't any funny activity going on. What they

don't know is, Latrice was already inside with Reyna

waiting, but Reyna had excused her self to go to the

lady's room. Chica decided to call the number back, seeing that Latrice still haven't arrived. Hey, Latrice answered, um is you still coming? Yes, darling I am actually outside, waiting for you to pull up. Oh, sorry Chica said, I'm outside I was already here. And I didn't see anybody, go in. Plus, this baby in my belly is starving, she said with a giggle. Oh, my goodness! Your pregnant, Latrice beamed with joy. Ok, I'm coming in now, I am about to be and aunty. Latrice said then ended the call. Chica looked at mark, she is already inside. Wow! She must do have me inside of her she laughed. Only a hood bitch thinks like that, word mark said. They exited the car and went inside, Chica was looking but she didn't notice any one. As, Chica looked she noticed Latrice waving her to come over. As Chica got closer she instantly became sick, that was the girl from the hotel. She kept walking towards her, she didn't want nothing to do with this chick. Oh, hello, sorry I am her to meet someone, I thought she was you waving. Chica said, oh hey me as well. They caught each other's voice, wait a minute chick said. She looked at mark and back at

185

the girl, are you Latrice? Latrice, shook her head yes. She stood up I knew it was a reason, at the hotel I asked you if I knew you from somewhere. Chica was stunned, omg, baby you aren't going to "fucking" believe this. He looked at her, then at Latrice he replied what? Do you know the hotel I almost gotten killed in? he screwed up his face, he said yea. What's up? Well this is the clerk, that almost died as well. Wow! She hugged Chica, I felt it, I did. Omg, Latrice rubbed her belly. You are so big; how many months are you? Seven she responded, now have a seat. I have my sister here, she is going to freak out about this. Matter fact here she is now, as Reyna walked towards the table. she went crazy, she started screaming and hugging Chica. Mark was more confused now than ever. Chica, mouth was wide open. Before she could finish, she asked what are you doing here? Long story short, this is my sister Latrice. We are here to meet her sister Chantel, Reyna said. Wait, you pregnant she asked? That fast realty slapped her in the face. She covered her mouth wait, no, then she looked at Latrice and back at

Chica that's your sister? This has to be a joke they

all said to each other, and king came walking in. he

was in P.A to handle business, before he took a flight

to go pay candy a visit. No one noticed him, until the

damn waited seated him right across from them. But

the only one noticed him was mark, they had beef

and he had been looking for him for years. I'm sorry

ladies I have to go handle something, he didn't

hesitate pulling out his Glock. Baby all yawl go to

the car, now! Wait, mark what happen? It was too

late, king turned around hearing his name. Reyna

188

and Chica noticed it was king. So, did Latrice

noooooo, she screamed. It was on death eyes. He let

off five rounds in king. He turned around and walked

out. Latrice pushed past everyone, she cried so hard.

Help him, please. That's my brother, somebody call

an ambulance. She screamed louder and louder,

Chica looked at Reyna, she said her brother. What

the "fuck" is going on here. Reyna looked at Chica,

it's so much deeper then you can imagine. Chica said

she can't turn my man in, I'm about to have his

child. What the fuck, I have to go. No, wait we can't

leave her. I have to go Chica said, fix this ray. Ill be in touched. She took off. Thank you all for reading part two, I hope you all enjoyed. Sequel Candy, had turned herself in to the prescient for everything. She found out king was dead, she didn't want to run no more. It had been three years since she saw little low, she was sent in a mental health institute. Low came to see her though, he wouldn't bring the baby. He would bring her pictures and presents, even let her speak to him. She was well now, and she was about to be released. Low was picking her up, and he

190

also was bringing little low. They even decided

giving their marriage another shot.

She really couldn't believe this day was finally

coming, and even though low was there for her. She

had falling for one of the guys that was also there.

His name was Danny, he was there because he found

out his brother was killed after trying to kill a lady

cop and he killed her husband who was also a cop.

But the male cop, used to rape him for way to long.

He was due to be released five days after her. She

smiled at the thought, but she wasn't to sure if she

191

could trust him. He like boys, but damn he cute she

thought to herself

Made in the USA
Columbia, SC
24 May 2022

60724639R00108